EDGE BOOKS™

PRO SPORTS
by the Numbers

PRO BASKETBALL
by the Numbers

by Todd Kortemeier

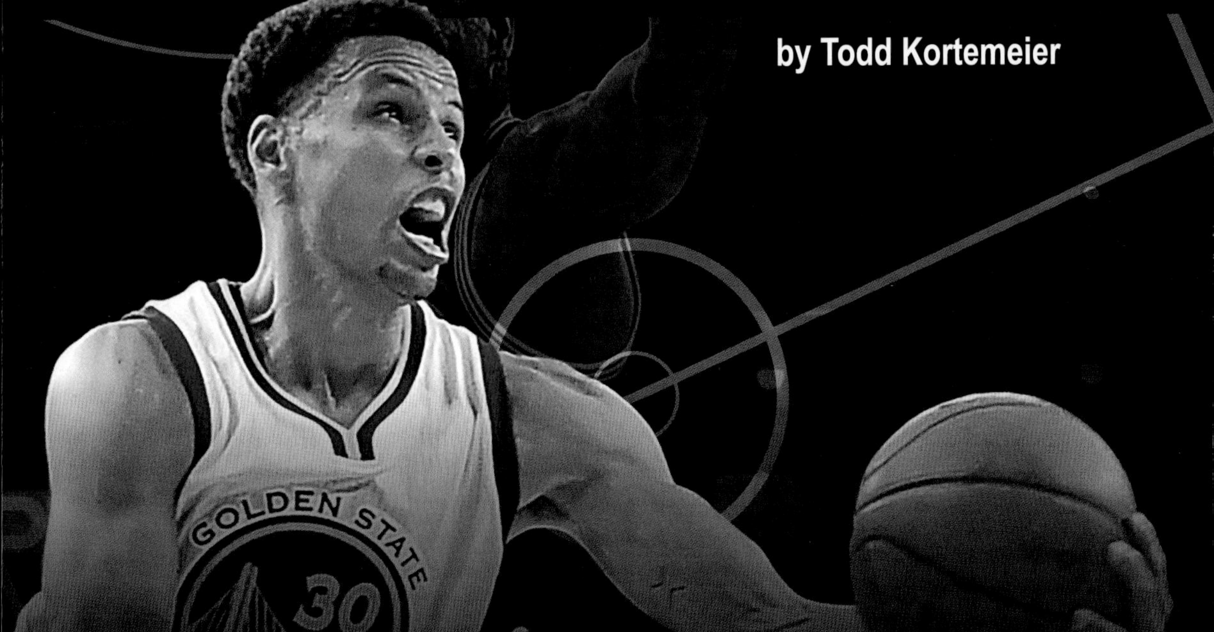

Consultant:
Stew Thornley, NBA Official Scorer and Sports Historian/Author

CAPSTONE PRESS
a capstone imprint

Edge Books are published by Capstone Press, 1710 Roe Crest Drive, North Mankato, Minnesota 56003
www.mycapstone.com

Library of Congress Cataloging-in-Publication Data
Cataloging-in-publication information is on file with the Library of Congress.

ISBN 978-1-4914-9058-7 (library binding)
ISBN 978-1-4914-9062-4 (paperback)
ISBN 978-1-4914-9066-2 (ebook PDF)

Editorial Credits
Patrick Donnelly, editor
Nikki Farinella, designer and production specialist

Photo Credits
AP Images: 4, Ben Margot, 19 (background), Bob Donnan/USA Today Sports Pool, cover (bottom), 1 (foreground), John Swart, 22 (left), Tony Dejak, cover (top); Carl Iwasaki/Sports Illustrated/Getty Images, 22 (right); Newscom: Aaron M. Sprecher/Icon SMI 952, 23 (left), Albert Pena/Cal Sport Media, 8–9 (foreground), 9 (top right), 19 (foreground), Charles Cherney/KRT, 5 (top right), Christopher Szagola/Cal Sport Media, 9 (bottom right), Doug Duran/TNS, 17 (middle bottom), Icon SMI 592/Icon SMI, 23 (right), Icon Sports Media 598/ Icon Sports Media, 24, John Fisher/Cal Sport Media, 20, John McDonough/Icon SMI, 17 (top), 28 (left), Kevin Sullivan/MCT, 28 (right), Lee K. Marriner UPI Photo Service, 17, Stephen M. Dowell/TNS, 17 (middle top), TMB/Icon SMI, 18 (foreground); Panacea_Doll/ iStockphoto/Thinkstock, 11 (top); Shutterstock Images: cover (right), 11 (bottom), 16, 22, 29, 360b, 26 (left), 26 (right), Alhovik, 9 (hoop), chrupka, 10–11, dean bertoncelj, 5 (top left), designelements, 15, Doug James, 18 (background), Eyes wide, 6–7, gst, 7, J. D. S., 14–15, Nelson Marques, 13 (top), Oleksii Sidorov, 16–17, Pavel Shchegolev, 4–5, 12–13, prophoto14, 21 (background), Torsak Thammachote, 8–9 (background), Ververidis Vasilis, 5 (bottom), Yuliyan Velchev, cover (background), 1 (background), 6–7, 13 (bottom), 21 (bottom), 26–27

Design Elements
Red Line Editorial (infographics), Shutterstock Images (perspective background, player silhouettes)

Printed in the United States of America in Mankato, Minnesota
102015   2015CAP

TABLE OF CONTENTS

THE ASSOCIATION

No other professional sport racks up the numbers like basketball. National Basketball Association (NBA) game scores commonly reach triple digits. The greatest players end their careers with tens of thousands of points. Even the heights of the players can be off the charts. Read on to discover some of the amazing numbers the game has to offer.

Timeline: Milestone Years of Basketball

1891
Dr. James Naismith invents the game of basketball.

1898
The first professional basketball league—the National Basketball League (NBL)—is founded. It folds during its sixth year.

1912
Baskets with open-bottom nets become popular.

1937
A new NBL is founded. This version is much more successful.

JOURNEY TO
30

The NBA was not always so stable. A lot of teams folded and moved in the early years of the league. It was a long journey as the league established the 30 solid teams it has today.

1949
The BAA and NBL merge and call the new league the National Basketball Association.

1962
Wilt Chamberlain scores 100 points in a game.

1998
Coach Phil Jackson and star guard Michael Jordan win their sixth title with the Chicago Bulls.

1954
The 24-second shot clock is invented.

1979
The league introduces a 3-point line.

2008
The Boston Celtics win their record 17th NBA championship, breaking a 22-year title drought.

1946
The Basketball Association of America (BAA) begins play.

1972
The Los Angeles Lakers' record 33-game winning streak ends.

THE HARDWOOD

Every NBA arena is different, but each **court** is the same size. Every measurement on the floor serves an important purpose.

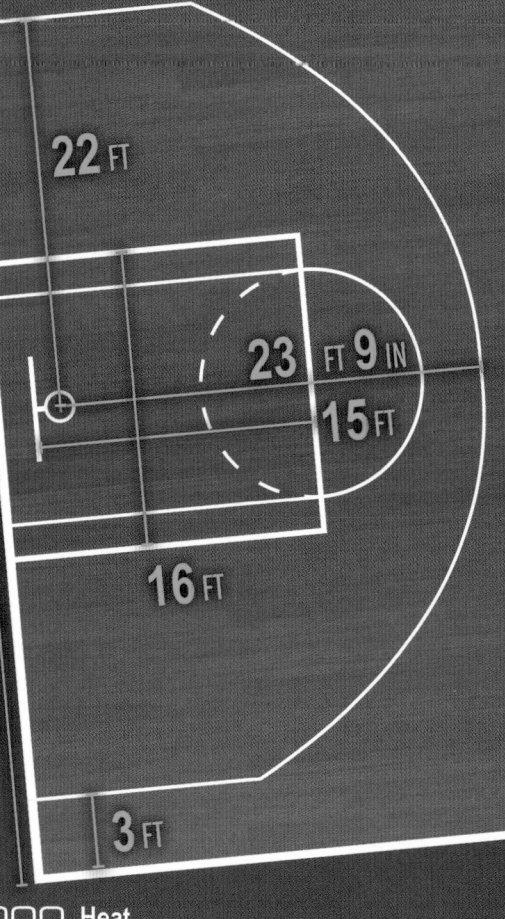

22 FT

50 FT

23 FT 9 IN

15 FT

16 FT

3 FT

WHEN NBA TEAMS BEGAN PLAYING IN THEIR CURRENT ARENAS

- 1968 Knicks
- 1971 Warriors
- 1988 Bucks, Kings, and Pistons
- 1990 Timberwolves
- 1991 Jazz
- 1992 Suns
- 1994 Cavaliers and Bulls
- 1997 Wizards
- 1999 Raptors, Pacers, Nuggets, Hawks, Lakers, and Clippers
- 2000 Heat
- 2002 Hornets and Spurs
- 2004 Grizzlies
- 2003 Rockets
- 1995 Trail Blazers and Celtics
- 1996 76ers
- 2001 Mavericks

court: the playing surface for basketball

Player Positions

1. POINT GUARD
2. SHOOTING GUARD
3. SMALL FORWARD
4. POWER FORWARD
5. CENTER

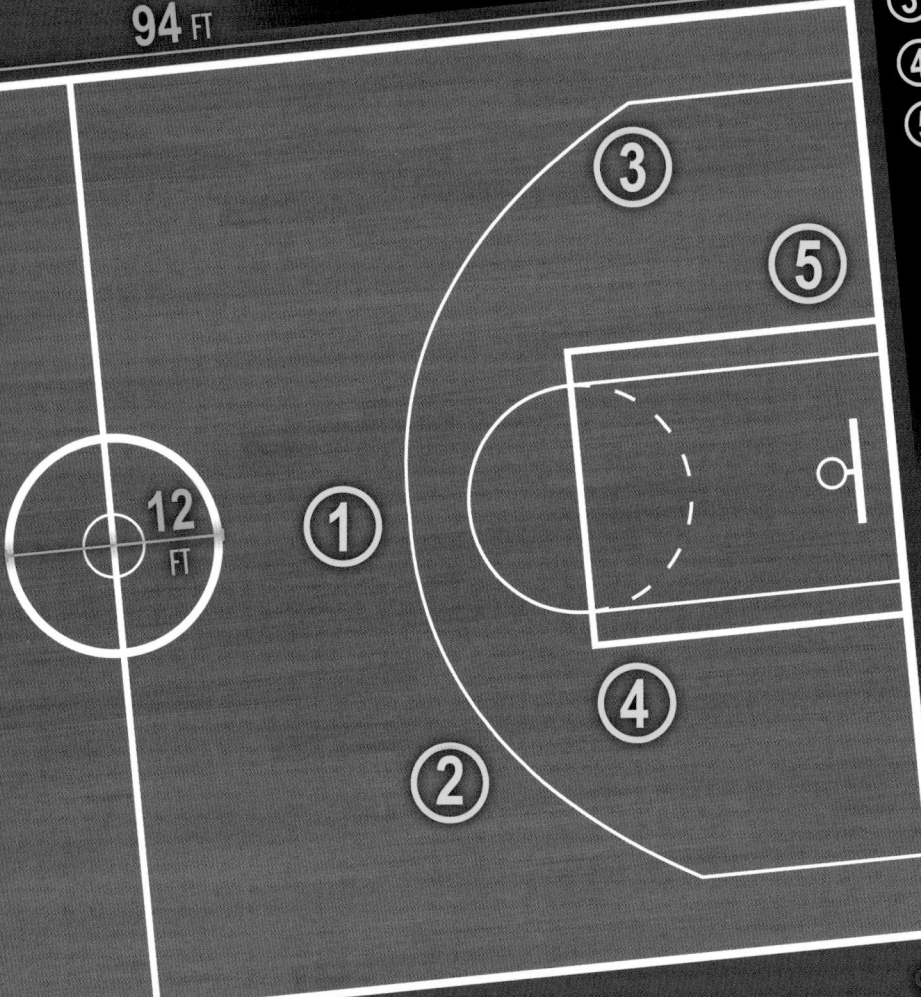

94 FT

12 FT

$30.20 cheapest average NBA ticket in 2014–15, New Orleans Pelicans

$53.98 average cost of an NBA ticket in 2014–15

$3,600 price per ticket for a New York Knicks courtside seat

$129.38 average cost of a Knicks ticket in 2014–15, the highest in the NBA

2005 Hornets

2008 Thunder

2010 Magic

2012 Nets

TICKET

THE ROCK

Dr. James Naismith invented basketball in 1891. In 1894 he asked the Spalding company to design a special ball for his new sport. The first basketball had laces on it; they weren't removed until 1937. The ball we know today has been basically unchanged since 1983. Each ball contains an inflated center covered in nylon. This inner sphere is then covered in rubber, and the leather outer panels are glued on.

3–4 SQUARE FEET
amount of leather per ball

52–56 INCHES
height a properly inflated ball will bounce when dropped from 6 feet

3,200 YARDS
length of nylon thread used on the ball's inner bladder

9 number of balls each team provides for pregame warm-ups

29.5–29.75 INCHES

72 number of balls issued to each team at the start of the season

7.5–8.5 POUNDS PER SQUARE INCH
air pressure of an NBA game ball

OFFICIAL GAME BALL

Adam Silver
COMMISSIONER

NBA

9 IN

2 MONTHS
time needed to break in a
new ball before game use

18 IN

100.5
average number of times Michael
Carter-Williams touched the ball
per game during the 2014–15
season, which led the NBA

2
number of balls
that can fit in
the hoop at the
same time

SPALDING

SPALDING

THE WORLD OF
BASKETBALL

Basketball first became popular in the United States, where it was invented. But in time the rest of the world has caught on. It's now one of the world's most popular sports. And players from around the world have a big influence on the NBA.

2014–15 NBA Players

22.4% International Players

United States 77.6%

215 number of countries with access to NBA games on TV or online

Canada 12

United States **349** PLAYERS

Haiti 1

Dominican Republic 2

Mexico 1

Jamaica 1

U.S. Virgin Islands 1

Senegal 1

Venezuela 1

Brazil 7

Argentina 3

1 number of international teams in the NBA, the Toronto Raptors. The Memphis Grizzlies formerly played in Vancouver, Canada.

N W E S

In 1990 the Utah Jazz and Phoenix Suns met in Tokyo, Japan, for the first regular-season NBA game outside of North America. The league has been back to Japan and also visited the United Kingdom and Mexico for regular-season games since then.

MAP KEY

A. Slovenia: 3
B. Croatia: 2
C. Serbia: 1
D. Greece: 2
E. Macedonia: 1
F. Montenegro: 3
G. Bosnia and Herzegovina: 3
H. Italy: 4
I. Switzerland: 2
J. Spain: 5
K. France: 10
L. United Kingdom: 2
M. Germany: 2
N. Sweden: 2
O. Poland: 1
P. Lithuania: 2
Q. Ukraine: 1
R. Georgia: 1
S. Turkey: 4
T. Israel: 2
U. Democratic Republic of the Congo: 1
V. Republic of the Congo: 1
W. Cameroon: 2
X. Nigeria: 1

Russia
4

47
number of languages in which NBA programming is broadcast

6
number of international players in the 2015 All-Star Game

Australia
8

New Zealand
1

BASKETBALL

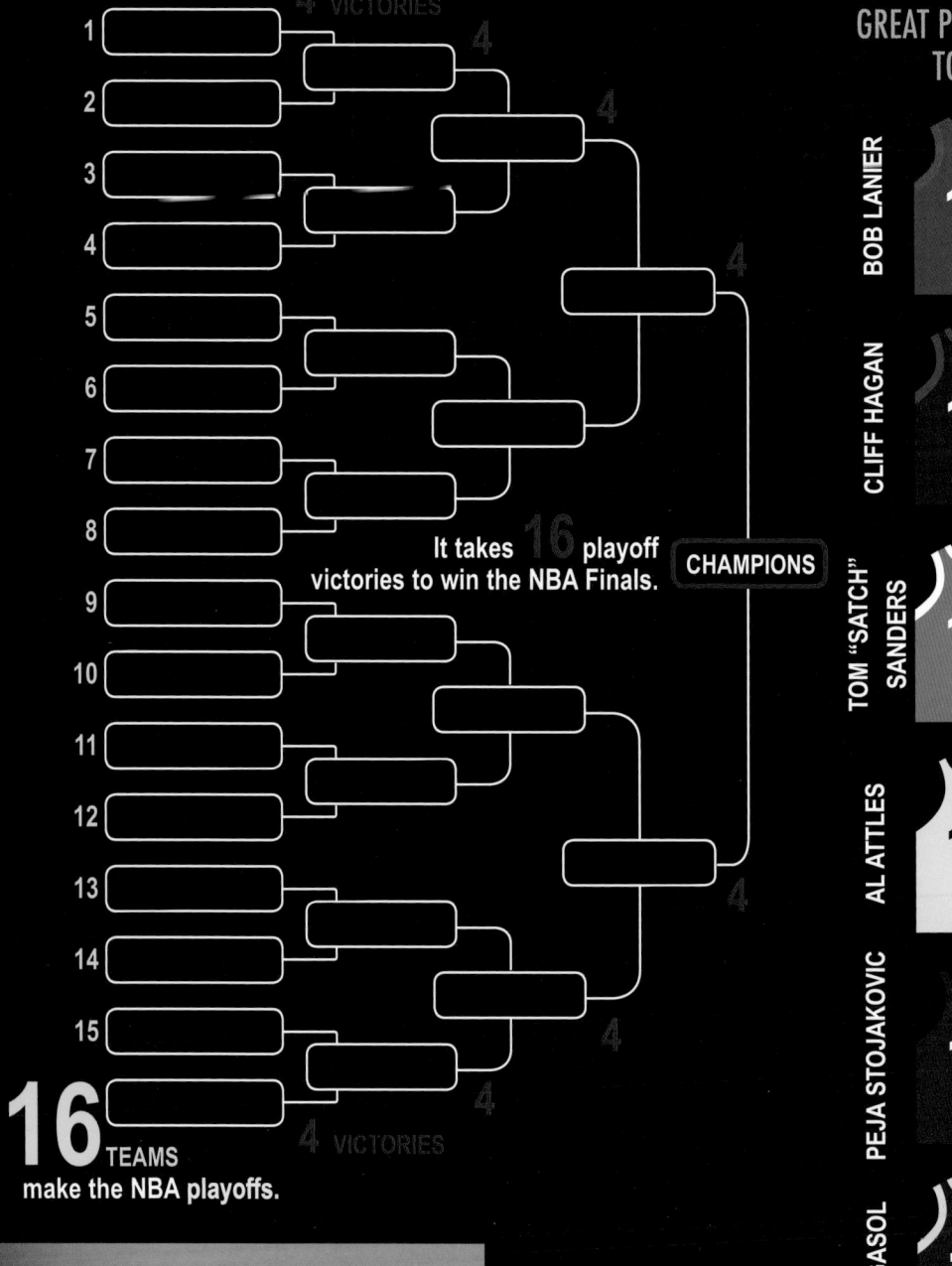

4 VICTORIES

1
2
3
4
5
6
7
8

4

4

4

It takes 16 playoff victories to win the NBA Finals.

CHAMPIONS

4

9
10
11
12
13
14
15

4

16 TEAMS
make the NBA playoffs.

4 VICTORIES

GREAT PLAYERS
TO WEAR

BOB LANIER — 16

CLIFF HAGAN — 16

TOM "SATCH" SANDERS — 16

AL ATTLES — 16

PEJA STOJAKOVIC — 16

PAU GASOL — 16

playoffs: the tournament held after
the regular season to crown the
NBA champions

12

BY THE 16s

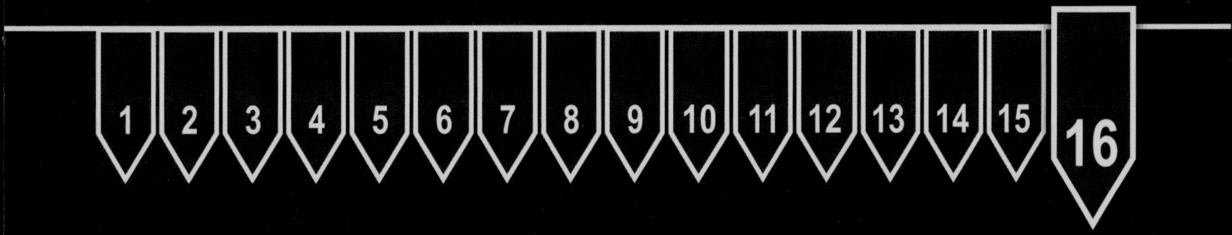

1 2 3 4 5 6 7 8 9 10 11 12 13 14 15 **16**

number of NBA championships for the Lakers

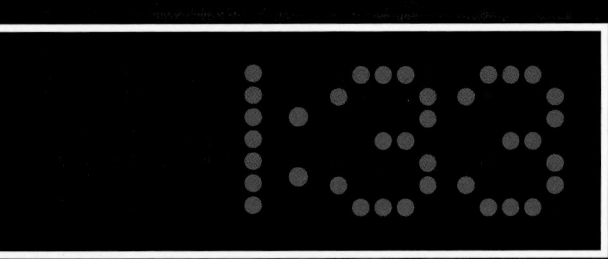

16 POINTS
scored by Isiah Thomas in the final 93 seconds of regulation of a 1984 playoff game to force overtime

16 FEET
width of the "key"

regulation: the scheduled time period of a basketball game; in the NBA it lasts 48 minutes
overtime: an extra period played to determine a winner if regulation ends in a tie
key: the painted area under the basket; also known as the "lane"

24 SECONDS THAT CHANGED THE GAME

The NBA of the 1950s didn't much resemble the high-scoring, high-flying sport we know today. Games were often boring and featured little action. The shot clock helped change that forever. Teams could no longer hold the ball to kill time. They had 24 seconds to shoot. If they didn't get a shot off, the referees blew the whistle and gave the ball to the other team.

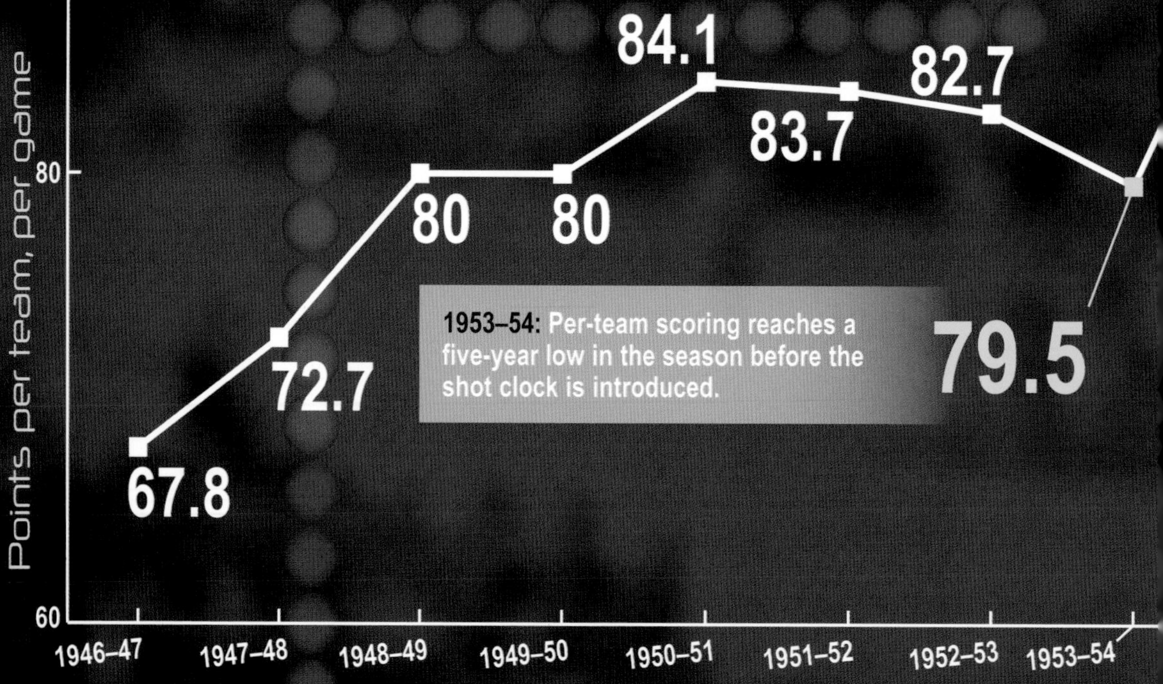

Points per team, per game

84.1

83.7

82.7

80

80

72.7

1953–54: Per-team scoring reaches a five-year low in the season before the shot clock is introduced.

79.5

67.8

1946–47   1947–48   1948–49   1949–50   1950–51   1951–52   1952–53   1953–54

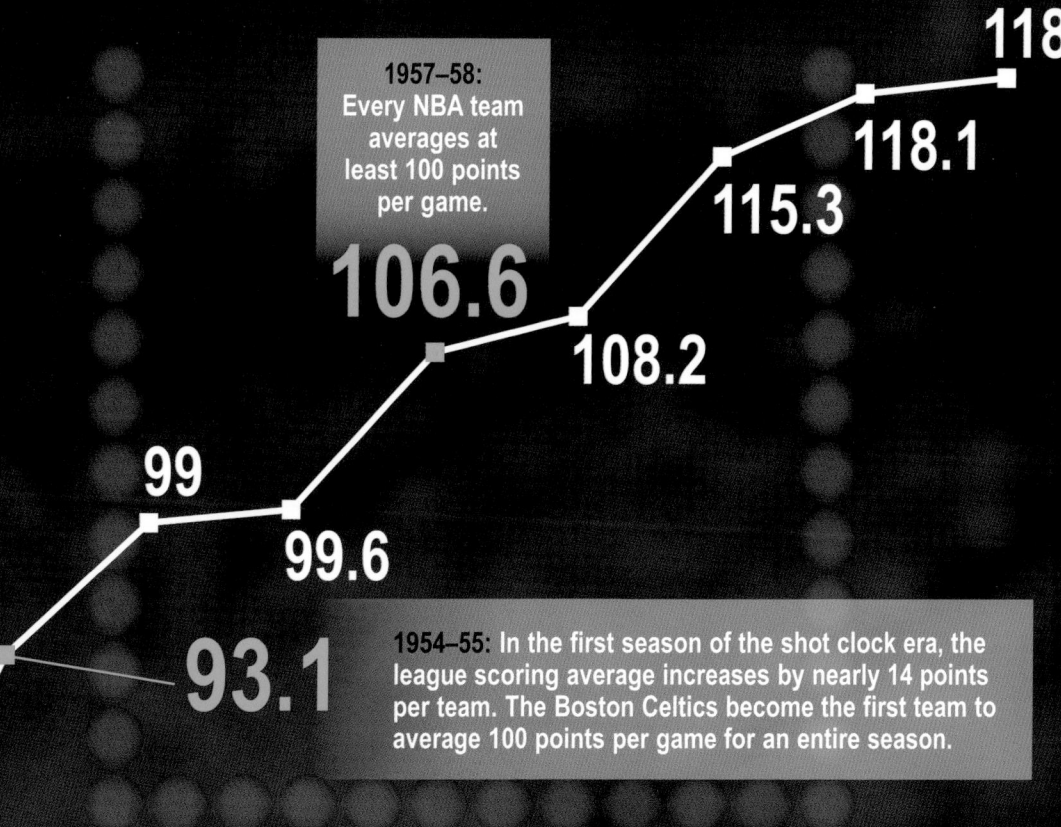

1957–58: Every NBA team averages at least 100 points per game.

118.8

118.1

115.3

106.6

108.2

99

99.6

93.1

1954–55: In the first season of the shot clock era, the league scoring average increases by nearly 14 points per team. The Boston Celtics become the first team to average 100 points per game for an entire season.

Before the 1954–55 season, teams with less talent could hold the ball and keep it away from their more skilled opponents. Danny Biasone, owner of the Syracuse Nationals, had an idea to fix this problem. Teams should have a set amount of time to get a shot off. But how much time? Biasone used the following formula:

$$\frac{120 \text{ shots/game}}{48 \text{ minutes}} = 24 \text{ seconds}$$

He estimated that in an exciting game, teams combined for approximately 120 shots. He then divided the number of shots into the length of the game—48 minutes, or 2,880 seconds. The result was 24 seconds.

| 1954–55 | 1955–56 | 1956–57 | 1957–58 | 1958–59 | 1959–60 | 1960–61 | 1961–62 |

THE LONG AND SHORT OF IT

Shoe Size

SHAQUILLE O'NEAL

LEAGUE AVERAGE
AVERAGE AMERICAN MAN

9

14.81

23

Basketball players are known for their height. The average NBA player today is 6 feet 7 inches tall. But some players are anything but average.

Average height of an NBA player

7

Feet

6' 4"

6' 5"

6' 6"

6' 7"

6

1950–51   1954–55   1962–63   1980–present

TODAY'S AVERAGE NBA PLAYER IS 3 INCHES TALLER AND 23 POUNDS HEAVIER THAN THE AVERAGE PLAYER IN 1951.

10 ft

9 ft

10 feet: height of an NBA hoop

7 feet 7 inches: Manute Bol (1985–1995, 2,086 career **blocked shots**)

6 feet 8: LeBron James (2003–, 4-time NBA Most Valuable Player)

6 feet 3: Stephen Curry (2009–, 2015 NBA Most Valuable Player)

6 feet 7: average height of an NBA player in 2014–15

5 feet 9: average height of an American man

5 feet 3: Tyrone "Muggsy" Bogues (1987–2001, 6,726 career **assists**)

assist: to pass the ball to a teammate who then makes a shot

blocked shot: when a shot is prevented from getting to the basket by a player knocking it out of the air

8 ft · 7 ft · 6 ft · 5 ft · 4 ft · 3 ft · 2 ft · 1 ft · 0 ft

THE RISE OF WOMEN'S BASKETBALL

In 1996 the NBA announced the creation of the Women's National Basketball Association (WNBA). The league began play the next year. Nearly two decades later, the WNBA is home to the best women's basketball players in the world.

FIRST YEAR **1997**

12 TEAMS

34 GAMES IN REGULAR SEASON

3-POINT LINE
22 feet at the **baseline**,
22 feet, 1 3/4 inches around the arc

BALL CIRCUMFERENCE
28.5–29 INCHES

QUARTER LENGTH **10** MINUTES

AVERAGE PLAYER HEIGHT **6** FEET

2015 SCORING LEADER
Elena Delle Donne, 23.4 points per game

ALL-TIME LEADING SCORER
Tina Thompson, 7,488 points (496 games)

WNBA

baseline: the end line on a basketball court, running sideline to sideline behind each basket

1892
James Naismith's original rules for basketball are adapted for women at Smith College.

2000
The Houston Comets win their fourth straight WNBA title.

1996
The American Basketball League (ABL) debuts. The league folds after 2 1/2 seasons.

1976
Women's basketball makes its debut at the Summer Olympics in Montreal, Canada.

1953
The United States wins gold at the first Women's World Basketball Championships.

Key Dates in Women's Basketball History

FIRST YEAR **1946**
(as the BAA)

30 TEAMS

82 GAMES IN REGULAR SEASON

3-POINT LINE
22 feet at the baseline,
23 feet, 9 inches around the arc

BALL CIRCUMFERENCE
29.5–29.75 INCHES

QUARTER LENGTH **12** MINUTES

AVERAGE PLAYER HEIGHT **6** FEET **7** INCHES

2014–15 SCORING LEADER
Russell Westbrook, 28.1 points per game

ALL-TIME LEADING SCORER
Kareem Abdul-Jabbar,
38,387 points (1,560 games)

NBA

19

AT THE LINE

Players are awarded **free throws** after **fouls** in certain situations. These **uncontested** shots can make a huge difference in the outcome of a game.

Career free-throw shooting percentage

BEST EVER Steve Nash, .904*
WORST EVER Andre Drummond, .397**
2014–15 LEAGUE AVERAGE .750

*minimum 1,200 attempts
**minimum 500 attempts

TOP PERFORMANCES

28 most free throws made in a game, Wilt Chamberlain (1962) and Adrian Dantley (1984)

39 most free-throw attempts in a game, Dwight Howard (2012 and 2013)

24 most free throws made in a game without a miss, Dirk Nowitzki (2011)

97 most free throws made in a row, Micheal Williams (3/24/93 to 11/9/93)

3.5 FEET height of the backboard

Points Scored in 2014-15

17.1% FREE THROWS

23.5% 3-POINT SHOTS

59.3% 2-POINT SHOTS

10 FEET height of the hoop

15 FEET distance from the free-throw line to the backboard

---

free throw: an uncontested shot taken from a line 15 feet from the basket
foul: a rules violation committed against a player of the opposing team

uncontested: open or unguarded
backboard: a glass rectangle behind the hoop and net

FROM
DOWNTOWN

A 3-pointer can get a losing team back in the game quickly. Having a player who can score from way downtown—that is, a long way from the basket—when the team needs it most can be huge. The 3-point line was first used in the American Basketball League in 1961. The NBA didn't adopt it until 1979.

19 INCHES
distance the NBA moved the line toward the hoop in 1994. The league 3-point percentage didn't change much, but attempts increased. The line was moved back to its original position in 1997.

TOP PERFORMANCES

9 most 3-pointers made in a game without a miss, Latrell Sprewell (2003) and Ben Gordon (2006 and 2012)

13 most consecutive 3-pointers made, Brent Price (1/15/1996 to 1/19/1996) and Terry Mills (12/4/1996 to 12/7/1996)

286 most 3-pointers made in a season, Stephen Curry (2014–15)

12 most 3-pointers made in a game, Kobe Bryant (2003) and Donyell Marshall (2005)

Heat map for Stephen Curry's long-distance shooting in 2014–15

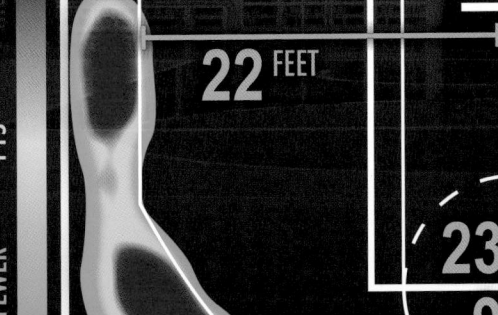

MORE
PTS
FEWER

22 FEET

23 FEET
9 INCHES

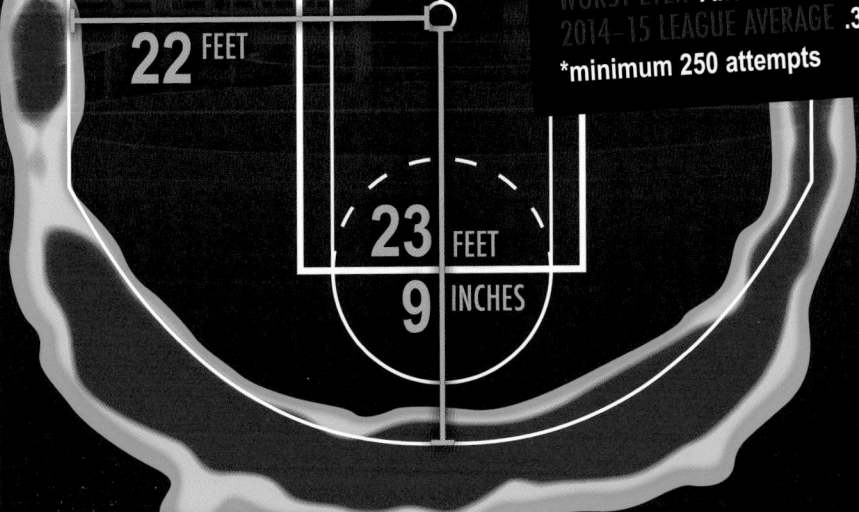

Career 3-point shooting percentage

BEST EVER **Steve Kerr, .454***
WORST EVER **Andre Miller, .217***
2014–15 LEAGUE AVERAGE **.350**

*minimum 250 attempts

THE DUNK

5-foot-7-inch Spud Webb wins the NBA dunk contest, the shortest player ever to do so.

1976

Jullus "Dr. J" Erving takes off from the free-throw line (15 feet) to win.

2008

While wearing a Superman cape, Dwight Howard becomes the tallest player to ever win, at 6 feet 11 inches.

1988

Michael Jordan wins the contest in front of his hometown fans in Chicago.

ARTISTS

Nate Robinson (only 5 feet 9 inches tall) dunks over Spud Webb to win.

In 1976 the American Basketball Association (ABA) held a **dunk** contest. The ABA later folded but some of its teams joined the NBA. The dunk contest also survived the collapse of the ABA. The NBA has hosted a dunk contest during its All-Star weekend since 1984. It is an opportunity for the league's high-flying experts to show what they can do.

2011

Blake Griffin jumps over a car (57.3 inches high) parked in the lane for the winning dunk.

dunk: to jump and throw the ball down directly through the hoop

THE BIG DIPPER GOES FOR 100

In 1962 Wilt Chamberlain was already one of the most dominant players in the game. On March 2 of that year, his Philadelphia Warriors faced the New York Knicks. That night Chamberlain did something that no NBA player has ever come close to matching—before or since. The man called "The Big Dipper" scored 100 points in one game.

WARRIORS	FIELD GOALS MADE	FIELD GOALS ATTEMPTED	FREE THROWS MADE	FREE THROWS ATTEMPTED	POINTS
Arizin	7	18	2	2	16
Meschery	7	12	2	2	16
CHAMBERLAIN	36	63	28	32	100
Rodgers	1	4	9	12	11
Attles	8	8	1	1	17
Larese	4	5	1	1	9
Conlin	0	4	0	0	0
Ruklick	0	1	0	2	0
Luckenbill	0	0	0	0	0
Totals	63	115	43	52	169

SCORE BY QUARTERS	1	2	3	4	FINAL
Philadelphia	42	37	46	44	169
New York	26	42	38	41	147

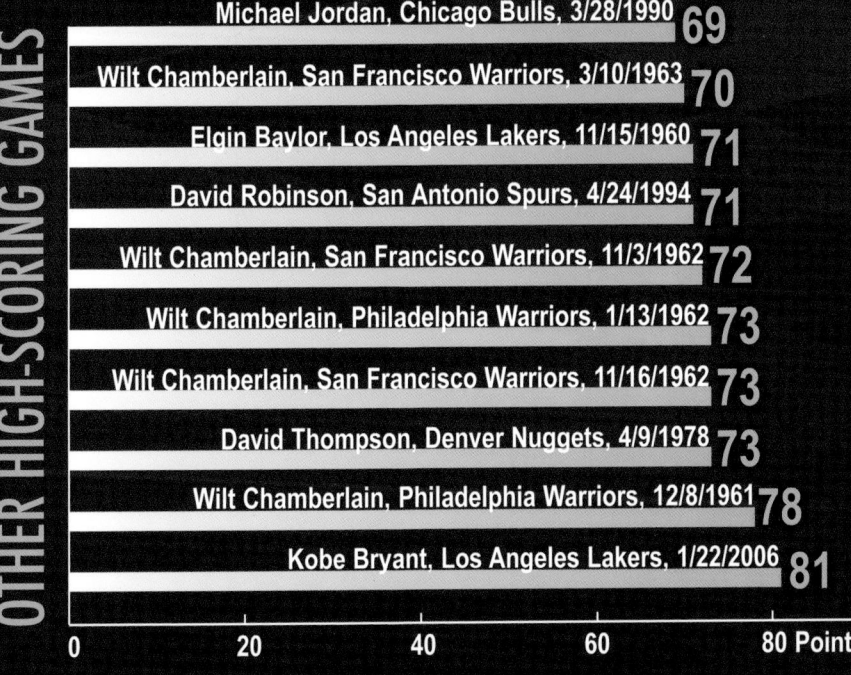

OTHER HIGH-SCORING GAMES

- Michael Jordan, Chicago Bulls, 3/28/1990 — 69
- Wilt Chamberlain, San Francisco Warriors, 3/10/1963 — 70
- Elgin Baylor, Los Angeles Lakers, 11/15/1960 — 71
- David Robinson, San Antonio Spurs, 4/24/1994 — 71
- Wilt Chamberlain, San Francisco Warriors, 11/3/1962 — 72
- Wilt Chamberlain, Philadelphia Warriors, 1/13/1962 — 73
- Wilt Chamberlain, San Francisco Warriors, 11/16/1962 — 73
- David Thompson, Denver Nuggets, 4/9/1978 — 73
- Wilt Chamberlain, Philadelphia Warriors, 12/8/1961 — 78
- Kobe Bryant, Los Angeles Lakers, 1/22/2006 — 81

0   20   40   60   80 Points

50.4 Chamberlain's per-game scoring average in 1961–62, That is still an NBA record.

31.6 Walt Bellamy's per-game scoring average in 1961–62. He finished second in the scoring race.

36 field goals (still an NBA record)

63 field goal attempts (still an NBA record)

28 OF **32** free-throw totals; at .875 it was much higher than his career percentage of .511

PHILADELPHIA WARRIORS 169, NEW YORK KNICKS 147
3/2/1962, at Hershey, Pennsylvania
Attendance: **4,124**

Most points in a game by two teams combined

370 Detroit (186) at Denver (184) in triple overtime, 12/13/1983

337 San Antonio (171) at Milwaukee (166) in triple overtime, 3/6/1982

320 Golden State (162) at Denver (158), 11/2/1990

field goal: a shot that is not a free throw

THE BEST OF THE BEST

CELTICS vs. LAKERS

The Boston Celtics and the Los Angeles Lakers are two of the NBA's most storied franchises. But who comes out on top? Compare their all-time accomplishments, from their humble beginnings through the 2014–15 season.

1946–47 — First season — **1947–48**
(as the NBL's Minneapolis Lakers)

3,173 — Wins — **3,218**

2,223 — Losses — **2,069**

52 — Playoff appearances — **60**

17 — Championships — **16**

27 — Hall of Famers — **21**

1995–96 CHICAGO BULLS

The Celtics and Lakers might be the two greatest franchises of all time. But the Chicago Bulls put together the most amazing single season in NBA history. The Bulls went 72–10 during the 1995–96 season. No NBA team has won more games in one year. The Bulls also lost only three games in four playoff series en route to winning the NBA title.

GAME 82
(4/21/1996)

GAME 75
The Bulls lose their first home game all season; they finish 39–2 at home.

GAME 54
The Bulls lose their third game in February, their most in any month.

GAMES 27–44
The Bulls win 18 games in a row, including every game in January 1996.

2
All-Star players (Michael Jordan and Scottie Pippen)

105.2
points per game (No. 1 in the NBA)

92.9
points allowed per game (No. 3 in the NBA)

3
future Hall of Famers on the team (Jordan, Pippen, and Dennis Rodman)

WINS

LOSSES

GAME 1
(11/3/1995)

TOP PERFORMERS

Calendar Month					
1	2	3	4	5	6
7	8	9	10	11	12	13
14	15	16	17	18	19	20
21	22	23	24	25	26	27
28	29	30	31	1	2	3

Calendar Month						
4	5	6	7	8		

57,446 MINUTES

time Kareem Abdul-Jabbar played in his career. That's 39 days, 21 hours, and 26 minutes of basketball!

2,973

number of 3-pointers Ray Allen made in his career. That's a combined distance of more than 13 miles, or half the distance of the Boston Marathon!

15,837

number of career field goals for Abdul-Jabbar. The closest active player, Kobe Bryant, would need more than 4,000 more to catch him.

9,787

career free throws made by longtime Utah Jazz star Karl Malone. That's nearly 28 miles of free throws, enough to get across the Great Salt Lake.

Double-Doubles and Beyond

If a player reaches double figures in two categories in a game (such as 10 or more points and assists), that player is said to have recorded a double-double. If a player reaches double figures in three categories (usually points, rebounds, and assists), that's a triple-double. It's a good indicator of players with a variety of skills. Here are some of the best at it.

181 most career triple-doubles, Oscar Robertson. Robertson had 41 of these during the 1961–62 season, in which he averaged a triple-double for the season. Robertson averaged 30.8 points, 12.8 rebounds, and 11.4 assists per game.

968 most career double-doubles, Wilt Chamberlain

4 number of players to have recorded a quadruple-double; Nate Thurmond, Alvin Robertson, Hakeem Olajuwon (twice), and David Robinson. All four reached double figures in points, rebounds, and assists. Thurmond, Olajuwon, and Robinson also reached double figures in blocked shots; Robertson did it in steals.

0 number of players to have ever recorded a quintuple-double, though WNBA star Tamika Catchings did it in high school

Glossary

assist (uh-SISST)—to pass the ball to a teammate who then makes a shot

backboard (BAK-bord)—a glass rectangle behind the hoop and net

baseline (BAYSS-line)—the end line on a basketball court, running sideline to sideline behind each basket

blocked shot (BLOKD SHOT)—when a shot is prevented from getting to the basket by a player knocking it out of the air

court (KORT)—the playing surface for basketball

dunk (DUHNGK)—to jump and throw the ball down directly through the hoop

field goal (FEELD GOHL)—a shot that is not a free throw

foul (FOUL)—a rules violation committed against a player of the opposing team

free throw (FREE THROH)—an uncontested shot taken from a line 15 feet from the basket

key (KEE)—the painted area under the basket; also known as the "lane"

overtime (OH-vur-time)—an extra period played to determine a winner if regulation ends in a tie

playoffs (PLAY-ofss)—the tournament held after the regular season to crown the NBA champions

regulation (reg-yuh-LAY-shuhn)—the scheduled time period of a basketball game; in the NBA it lasts 48 minutes

uncontested (uhn-kuhn-TEST-id)—open or unguarded

Read More

Adamson, Thomas K. *Basketball: The Math of the Game*. Kids Sports Math. Mankato, Minn.: Capstone Press, 2012.

Slade, Suzanne. *The Technology of Basketball*. High–Tech Sports. North Mankato, Minn.: Capstone Press, 2013.

Critical Thinking Using the Common Core

1. On pages 14 and 15 you learned about the history of the shot clock in the NBA. Why do you think NBA owners wanted to increase scoring in their games? (Integration of Knowledge and Ideas)

2. Nobody has come close to matching Wilt Chamberlain's 100-point game. But on that night Chamberlain also took more shots than any player has ever taken in an NBA game. His teammates wanted him to reach 100 points, so they passed him the ball more often. Does that make Chamberlain's feat less impressive in your opinion? Why or why not? (Key Ideas and Details)

Internet Sites

FactHound offers a safe, fun way to find Internet sites related to this book. All of the sites on FactHound have been researched by our staff.

Visit *www.facthound.com*

Type in this code: 9781491490587

Check out projects, games and lots more at
www.capstonekids.com

Index